I would like to thank my daugher, Elizabeth for her inspiration and design skills. She helped make this book a reality.

Hope you all enjoy!

Beach Etiquette

Author:
George H. Hutchinson III

Daughter & Co-author:
Elizabeth Ackmann

Illustrator:
Samantha Edwards

ISBN-13: 978-1979773386
ISBN-10: 1979773386

DEDICATION

To Janet, the Hutchies and the TI crew

I want to start out by saying I am a big fan of the beach.
I have been going to the Jersey shore since 1956 and
have many fond memories of running, playing in the sand,
body surfing, surfing and just relaxing on the beach.

If you are looking to kick back and relax, nothing beats a day on the beach.

Some people say the shore.
You actually drive to the shore and then you walk to the beach.
What follows are a few simple rules I call beach etiquette
that will allow you to enjoy your day just a little bit more.

1
Banner Beach Day – *Where Should We Sit?*

You wake up early in the morning and take a quick look out the window. The sun is shining brightly. It's going to be a banner beach day. You find yourself hurrying to eat breakfast and to complete the morning chores, the whole time thinking about stretching out along the water's edge. Your neighbors are packing up their beach chairs, coolers, towels and toys. Taking a quick glance down the street, you see a steady stream of people, all heading to the beach, like there's a finish line. Anxiously you think…"Look at all these people, getting a head start. The beach is going to be crowded today!" Finally, you're finished.

You pack, taking a mental inventory…
sandwiches
drinks
towels
blanket
beach chairs
beach tags

Do we have any balls or shovels for the kids to play with? Yep!

Did you bring money for ice cream? Of course!
Ok, let's get going. Everyone's ready to go. Anticipation grows.

You make your way up the street with your family in tow. You hit the top of the dunes.

It's high tide; everyone is packed together in the hot sand like sardines. You think,

"My God! Where are we going to sit?

Rule #1
The acceptable width from your fellow beach-goer is 5 feet more or less (preferably more). This will provide plenty of room for everyone to move around comfortably so that all can have a good time.

The latest fad you are seeing on the beach is tent spreading. Being from a large family, we end up

with a large crowd every weekend on the beach. For those bringing large tents, make sure you have the numbers to support it. Instead of trying to get a front row seat, look to set up your tent towards the back near the dunes. This should give you ample room to set up and enjoy your day.

The beach is public property to be shared and enjoyed by all. In choosing a place to sit you must respect all those who are sharing the beach with you. If you have young children, settle close to the lifeguard stand. Make sure you choose a spot that allows your whole party to relax comfortably with room for their blanket, coolers and chairs.

2
Blanket Encroachment

It's a beautiful sunny day. There you are, sitting in your
favorite chair, waves lapping over your ankles,
at the water's edge.

Well… with all the lounging you've done,
you surely deserve a nap!

You fold the chair and head back to your belongings for a long
stretch on the blanket. Sauntering up, you are overcome with
shock and exclaim in exasperation,

"What the hell happened?"

Your once pristine green-checkered blanket anchored down
by sandals and a now capsized water jug
… is covered with sand!

It looks like a bomb exploded… patterns of footprints, all
shapes and sizes crisscrossing the blanket
with grains of sand clinging to it like a magnet.

You look around, seeking an apologetic look or at least
someone with whom you can commiserate

…but a sea of blank faces stares back at you.

Rule #2
*A blanket on the beach is like a piece of furniture, take the few extra seconds to walk around it.
Treat it with respect and care. Would you run over someone's couch with shoes or sit on your
furniture at home, pockets filled with sand? I would think not!*

*A beach blanket, like a chair, is someone's property. Should you need to pass, take care to walk
around the perimeter. Should you want to sit or lie down on the blanket, before you do so, brush*

off any sand from your bathing suit or body. Turn around and sit down on the edge with your feet still in the sand. Once seated you can stretch out your legs, or lie down on your back, but always leave feet extended over the edge.

Don't forget to get a towel and roll it up for a pillow!

3
Eating Lunch

One of the true delights on a summer day is eating lunch on the beach… a seaside picnic. In the morning you decide between a packed lunch (sandwiches, a bag of chips and, of course, cookies)
or is today a coveted "Hot Dog Day?"

Those are the days you hike over the sand, baking in the mid-day sun, to a long line at your beloved Hot Dog vendor. As you hop back and forth from one foot to the other until numbness replaces the heat, you make a mental note to remember to wear your sandals the next time.

Waiting seems remarkably endless; you begin to agree with your kids' raised voices,
Could they order faster?

Now that you have your spread, there are a few things that you must watch out for
while enjoying your little picnic…

Seagulls!

The "flying rats" are circling overhead looking for their next prey. You notice your wife seated on the blanket, in the approach mode, about to take a bite. But too late! Before you can even warn her, one of these scavengers has swooped down and grabbed the sandwich right out of her hand. She shrieks, neighbors jump up to see what happened, children start crying and you shake your head…

not again.

Rule #3
Always keep your sandwich or any food you are holding in your hands covered. Should you drop food while eating, pick it up, otherwise you are inviting seagulls to lunch with you.

Use a sandwich wrapper, a napkin, or for kids to ensure a meal in peace, cover their heads with a towel. Once you are done eating, gather all the meal's remnants and deposit them in the nearest trash can. They are usually located next to a beach entrance, in front of the dunes for all to find.

4
Oh, the Seagulls

Remember in the last chapter, we spoke about having to eat lunch with a towel over your head?

This is a true defensive measure.

In the beginning of each summer season you can relax and enjoy a sandwich or grab a handful of pretzels in the open air while on the beach. As the summer progresses the seagull militarization gains momentum.

Suddenly, laughter erupts on your right. As you glance over to find the source, you see both children and adults tossing bread, chips and other food scraps to a cluster of seagulls. Pointing and shouting with their friends, they sling another potato chip, this time within two feet of your chair. With horror an airstrike begins. You watch helplessly as 12 or more seagulls plummet toward the salty chip.

Didn't they ever see the movie "The Birds?"
Each person caught throwing food to seagulls should be locked in a room and
forced to watch that movie a minimum of 10 times.

Wings flapping, their sharp cawing rises in the late summer, overweight gulls fight over their mid-day snack.

Irate…

you reflect on the urge to feed those people to the seagulls.

Rule #4
Feeding seagulls is not acceptable. Parents, if you see your children throw food at the seagulls, get up and explain to them that there are other people on the beach. Respect the seagulls' habitat and fellow beach goers right to relax without the threat of squabbling dive bombs.
And to those adults who continue to throw food at seagulls, shame on you. You are not setting a good example… mind your manners.

The beach is the natural habitat of the Herring Gulls, the quintessential gray-and-white, pink-legged 'seagulls'. Their diet includes marine life and insects, but does not include the remnants of a family size potato chip bag or a two-year-olds abandoned peanut butter and jelly sandwich. Besides avoiding to feed them for entertainment… if food is dropped, pick it up and throw it away.

5
The Passing Lane

There is so much excitement at the beach, so many things to do. For many, this time is a treasured family vacation, well-earned retreat or friend reunion. For some, it is an annual tradition and for others, their first time.

People come from all over to enjoy the seaside air in various ways: picnics, body surfing,
kite flying or just relaxing.
Shoobie or veteran, you'll hear them yell "let's race to the water!"

Sitting comfortably on the beach, entrenched in a good book, caught up in conversation or just sunning yourself…
it happens.

Whoosh - Your head snaps up.

A herd comes rushing by, sand flying, water splashing, someone's knee hits your chair,

"Sorry, man."

The serene moment you were once caught up in, suddenly broken. Your thoughts jolted,

"What in the heck was that?"

Rule #5
When you are around a group of people --- slow down, walk, don't run. Time at the beach is for everyone to enjoy, you are not the only ones there. Pass the word.

Be conscious of a person's right to privacy and relaxation. Everyone can admit to being a little tornado at times, caught up in the excitement. Going for a quick dip or racing to the water? Walk

to where the path is clear, and then blow the starting whistle. To play a game, note where others have their nets and bocce set up. There is plenty of room to run, jump and flop by the water's edge, in the dry sand, or by the dunes.

6
Having a Catch

The faint sounds of teen laughter are heard in the distance.
"Hey, anybody bring a ball? Let's play run the bases."

You reflect back on your memories on this same beach, where
you once developed your slide;
head first… reaching, hook slide… dragging the back foot.

What great shape you were in! Running through the sand,
zigzagging, dodging the tag, until your legs felt like lead.
As the game ended there was a massive sprint into the water.
Ahhh, the perfect cool off.

You glance over to watch the game, laying out the bases you
note that second base is awfully close to where you are sitting.
The kids' side talk is disrupted by a swift plastic smack of the
bat's contact with the whiffle ball.
Going high, high, higher you forget your placement and think
- Nice hit.

The ball starts its descent, a twelve year old backs up hurriedly,
arms outstretched.
"Got It!"

Just passed second base -- he topples over you.
Knocking off your glasses, the book from your hand and the
drink from your koozie.

"Sorry, Mister."

Rule #6
Playing catch, running the bases or volleyball should be done with ample room, in the dry sand by the dunes or along the waters' edge. If you are close to other vacationers, do not use the people around you as bases, a foul line or homerun territory. Find your own little sweet spot to learn, laugh and create memories without having to call "Heads up!"

On a crowded beach day, walk a few blocks. A rule of thumb for your field is sixty feet around. Homerun territory is usually the dunes, but to prevent a lost ball, an ace tip is to play against the wind.

7
Splish, Splash I Was Taking a... Run

A morning run with a friend can be a relaxing habit. Anywhere
from 3-5 miles, gives you time to talk, catch up on gossip and
laugh at stupid jokes.

What a great feeling, setting your pace along the water's edge.
No music needed, the ocean is your stereo with rolling waves
breaking, a nice breeze blowing and plenty of scenery to take
in.

The beach run offers the perfect opportunity to acknowledge a
nice bikini or two, something that is rare on your hometown's
tree-lined streets.

Later in the day, your run complete, the sun's intense rays caused
you to move your chair to the shoreline.
Eyes closed, feet covered in cool, wet sand, you hear the familiar
rhythmic, smack, smack, smack.
Someone's on their afternoon run.

Wooosh!
A Niagara of sand-filled water covers you.

You cry out "Hey buddy, is this the passing lane?"

Rule #7
*Don't run recklessly past people. This complaint is not directed at any age
category, although senior citizens may be excluded to some degree. If you are a parent of a quick
sprinter, or child, remind him or her to be mindful of other people. As for the seasoned jogger,
running on the beach can be enjoyed without encroaching on other people's right to relax and
enjoy their day.*

Running is good; running with awareness is better. The perfect time for a run on a crowded beach day would be at low tide, in the early morning or late afternoon, right before the lifeguards take their leave. These are also better times for your body as running in the mid-day heat can be dangerous to your health. If you choose to run in the early afternoon, make sure you are vigilant of the crowds, running children and slower moving adults.

8
Shake… Shake… Shake

With family on vacation, the early morning is the perfect time to sleep late or run out for a quick 18 holes. Schedule the first tee-off time and you can expect to return by 10:30-11, just in time to leave for the beach.

Your wife, the saint that she is, has lunches and towels packed and the kids white with sunscreen. The carriage is weighed down like a caravan with one or two babies inside and the blankets, chairs, drinks and snacks packed on top.

After a couple hours of kids playing in the sand and jumping in the waves, they are getting tired.
You yell out,

"Anyone ready for a nap?"

One by one, they lay down for a nap, sleeping by the water's edge, under the umbrella. This time is cherished, to relax with your kids …and to potentially recover, not only from last night, but also a bad golf game.

Whether lying there peacefully, enjoying a nap or relaxing on the blanket, nothing will jerk you,
or your sleeping children, back into reality

more than a sandstorm from the neighbor's blanket shake.

Rule #8
Shake your blanket in open space away from playing (or sleeping) children and fellow beachgoers. "Can I shake my rug out on you?" This would not be an acceptable question cleaning your house. Similarly, a beach blanket is nothing more than a rug laid down over a floor of sand.

When you are getting ready to leave the beach, remember that wind tends to carry things, especially sand. Carefully drag your blanket and other loose items to a section of the beach to shake, usually up by the dunes, where the sand won't wash over the people surrounding you.

9
Do You Like Good Music?

"Do you like good music…that sweet soul music?" Now… with the advent of portable audio systems and blue tooth speakers, everyone can customize a personal playlist for their perfect beach day. Most bring summer classics, tapping their feet to a beautiful melody, a great harmony or the latest catchy hook.

"Turn on the music!"

You glance at your neighbor and his group, give the polite nod, a signal for him to understand your family surrounds you, not to mention the seven under 7 year-olds playing in close vicinity.

Then… your ears begin to ring as the base thumps loudly. You just became an Atlantic City nightclub.

Thump… thump… thump...

Your head matches the beat,

Oh no… the other neighbor sees this as a chance to turn up their volume.

Dueling pianos may be popular at a bar, but on the beach dueling speakers are never acceptable.

Rule #9
Listen to music at a controlled volume on your speaker or opt for headphones to throw your own, personal concert. If you want to share music with a group of friends or family on the beach, make sure the music is acceptable for all ages and the volume is at a level so that people can converse, without yelling.

10
Why Do They Have Lifegaurds?

Oh, the water! After all isn't that what the beach is all about? Swimming past the breakers, diving through the waves, living the dream…in front of the lifeguard stand.

Lifeguards carry the responsibility of providing safety for anywhere from 200-300 people with only two or three sets of eyes. They deal with strong currents, riptides and crowds.

Wading in the water, you smile and clap as your kids come in and out, body surfing. You notice one or two people, a ways off, neglecting the lifeguard's whistle and sweeping arm waves to get out of the water.

Although they are just cooling off or peeing, they are still in the water, away from the designated swimming area. They've put all who choose to swim safely, in jeopardy. Now, one of the lifeguards has to leave their post and get the attention of the culprits to bring them back into the fold.

Speaking of peeing, it's the gullies where all the little kids go to relieve themselves,
even though you can usually walk to the nearest bathrooms.

Rule #10
Although you may know how to swim without supervision, when lifeguards are present always go in front of the stands. You could put others at risk because of your indiscretions. Lifeguards are there to protect all of us, don't make them waste time chasing after one person. If you see someone going in the water, remind him or her that they must swim in front of the lifeguards.

Most towns with lifeguards space the stands 3-5 blocks apart depending on the crowds. They also have designated beaches for surfing, kayaking and rafting. Use the guards' whistles as a honing beacon on where to go and what to do. If you see a red flag go up, be sure to exit the water immediately, as it means there is a life-threatening emergency. Yellow flag means to proceed with caution, there may be riptides.

11
Smoking Section

From cigars to cigarettes and the new ecigarettes, just about
everyone knows someone who smokes.
Whether you do or don't light up at the beach, where it's still
legal, it's widely done.
Like me, you may agree the back third of the cigar is the most
enjoyable.

As the 3:00 PM tide rolls up, you move the chairs up the dunes
and sit down and unwrap a cigar. You look around make sure
no one is in threat of inhaling the smoke and sit back to relax.

You begin to smell something familiar, a cigarette, and hear
the voice of the neighbor next to you within a couple feet.

It seems as though they thought your cigar was an invite to
come on over,

...is this the smoking section?

There is a cloud of smoke covering you and

...was that an ash?

Rule #11
*Whatever you light up, give ample space for wind to carry the smoke
away from your neighbors. Everyone who does smoke should be
responsible for disposal of any items associated with smoking. Pick up
after yourself and dispose of all tobacco remains. Matches or cigarette
butts should not be flicked into the ocean or inserted into the sand.
Enjoy your smoke, just don't forget to clean up.*

12
Who's the Trashman Around Here?

"Heyyy Ice Cream – Fudgyyy Wudgyy – Here"

It's the familiar call of the Fudgy Wudgy man, he may pass ten times but only when you have a craving for a cherry water ice or ice cream sandwich do your ears tune in.

As you walk to collect your frozen treat, accompanied by any child that has some claim to you, you begin to notice cans, chip bags and napkins from the lunch finished several hours ago littering the path.

On your walk back you assume the role as trash collector. Possibly you stumble upon an abandoned dollar along the path, making your citizen duty worth it.

Although everyone brings money and an appetite, not many think about the trash that can accumulate.

Don't let the dreaded walk to the bins through the hot sand deter you.

Rule #12
Collect your trash in a secure setting like a plastic bag, safe from the wind and running children. When you leave, assign someone to pick up all the debris and throw it in the trash receptacle. Place yourself in a home setting. If every neighbor picked up papers, cigarette butts and swept their sidewalks, the whole neighborhood would be clean. If everyone took the time to pitch in, the beach would always keep its pristine, glistening look.

Beach tags and day passes provide for a service to keep the beach clean. In the early hours of the morning a tractor passes, churning the sand and erasing the footsteps and sand castles made the day before. This money also provides trash cans and recycling cans on every block for beach goers to toss their daily waste. Be sure to use them.

13
Lead By Example

As everything is shaken and washed off and the toys are packed, the eventful day comes to an end. You reflect on all the ups and downs, from the temper tantrums and ball games to the peaceful naps and delicious hot dogs. Your kids and beach buddies know the routine as you strive to show good examples of beach behavior.

You take one last glance at the blanket next to yours and smile at your beach neighbor.

They're Shoobies afterall... someone just needs to educate them on proper beach etiquette.

It takes a few extra courtesy seconds to be mindful of others and to protect this great gift of 141 miles called the Jersey Shore. People come and go, but the beach remains and we should all work to preserve the beauty, share in the memories and pass this gift on for all.

Yes, you think, the Jersey Shore is a gift from God and we should treat it as such.

We must share and protect it with care, perhaps you should write a book about it...

Oh, and don't forget to wash the sand off your feet before you go into your house.

About the Author

George Hutchinson is a born and bred Jersey boy raised
in South Jersey, spending his summer's at the shore.